FINANCIAL FITNESS

WORKBOOK

THE OFFENSE, DEFENSE, AND
PLAYING FIELD OF PERSONAL FINANCE

Published by:

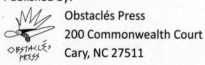

Obstaclés Press
200 Commonwealth Court
Cary, NC 27511

Visit our website at:
lifeleadership.com

ISBN: 978-0-9858020-6-6

First Edition, June 2013
15 14 13 12

Book design by Norm Williams, nwa-inc.com
Printed in the United States of America

PART I

BASICS

"THIS IS A FOOTBALL."

CHAPTER ONE

Why Do Some People Have Plenty of Money, While Others Constantly Struggle Financially?

Use the *Financial Fitness* book to fill in the blanks.

Financial fitness, like physical fitness, requires two things: _____ what to do, and taking _____ to do it.

The reason that some people have enough _____ , while others constantly struggle financially, is simply because those people have learned the principles of _____ _____ and consistently apply them—while others do not.

PRINCIPLE 1: It's not what you make but what you keep that determines financial success. Pay yourself first and save what you pay yourself.

How do you plan to apply this principle in your life?

_____

_____

CHAPTER TWO

Ascertaining What Money Really Means to You and Why It's Important to Be Financially Fit

Make _____ in order to enable your _____ and build your stewardship.
Start with the _____ !
What would you do to _____ the _____ if you could?

PRINCIPLE 2: Money is a gift. It has a specific use. This means that you have a stewardship. You are to use your money for something that matters, for your family and beyond.

How do you plan to apply this principle in your life?

_____

_____

Imagine you just inherited $10 million from a distant relative. What would you do? Think about the following questions and write down the things that you would now be able to do.

_____

_____

What will you do with your work or career?

_____

_____

How will you spend your time each day?

_____

_____

What do you really want to spend your time doing for the rest of your life?

_____

_____

Some people think they would quit work and watch television, but for the few who have actually been able to do this, such a focus has proven very unfulfilling. So, seriously, what would you want to do with the years ahead?

_____

_____

Would you stay in your current career? Switch to another? Build a business, or grow the one you already have?

_____

_____

Second, with whom do you want to spend more time?

_____

_____

What do you want to do with them? This is a hugely important question because it helps you see where your heart really is right now.

_____

_____

Next, what do you want to learn, experience, or do? Do you want to travel, learn to play a musical instrument or speak another language, or pursue a higher education or some other interest? Do you want to make a lot more money? Make a list.

_____

_____

Fourth, how would you use some of your money in the Faith area of your life?

_____

_____

What about Family?

_____

_____

Fun?

_____

_____

Freedom?

_____

_____

Finally, where do you want to donate some of your money—to a hospital, a school, your church, or somewhere else? This also helps you see where your heart really is and what you would like to do to improve the world.

_____

_____

This is a profound question: What would you do to change the world if you could?

_____

_____

The Dream and the Dread

The principles of financial fitness are simple, but not easy. Knowing the reasons *why* you want to be financially fit will help you stay motivated. People are motivated by either pleasure or pain (the "dream" or the "dread"). In order to form a clear picture in your mind of exactly what you want so that you can be focusing on your dream, vision, and life purpose, it can sometimes be helpful to consider what you would like to avoid: the negative consequences, or "dreads," of being financially flabby. Below, list the negative consequences, or "dreads," that you would like to avoid and then use those to create statements that correspond with your life vision. For example, if you want to avoid having poor credit and dealing with creditors calling and writing all of the time because you can't keep up with your payments, your dream affirmation could be something like, "I have perfect credit and always pay my bills on time."

The Dread

1. _____
2. _____
3. _____
4. _____
5. _____
6. _____
7. _____
8. _____
9. _____
10. _____

The Dream

1. _____
2. _____
3. _____
4. _____
5. _____
6. _____
7. _____
8. _____
9. _____
10. _____

What Are Your Priorities?

Place the following categories in the order of your personal priority:

Hobbies/Fun	Extended Family	Finances	God/Faith
Work	Friends	Health/Fitness	Your Children
Your Country	Helping Others	Your Spouse	Your Local Community

1. _____
2. _____
3. _____
4. _____
5. _____
6. _____
7. _____
8. _____
9. _____
10. _____
11. _____
12. _____

Look back over your calendar for the last month. Next to each item above, write down the approximate time spent on that priority.

Does the time spent in each category line up with your priorities? In what areas do you want to focus more of your time?

_____

_____

What obstacles are keeping you from applying the proper focus and spending sufficient time on your top priorities?

_____

_____

If you had a large source of continual passive income, what would change regarding the time and focus spent on your priorities?

_____

_____

CHAPTER THREE

How to Begin Getting Financially Fit

Instead of just doing _____ reading, you need to become a _____ reader. It isn't enough to simply understand a principle; you must _____ it in everyday life.

Step one to paying yourself first is to open a savings account. If you already have a savings account, open another one for this step. This account should be treated as sacred, as it will create the capital you need to eventually take you from survival to success.

Goal: I will open my savings account by _____ .
                                                              (date)
Completed: _____ .
                        (date)

Step two is to create a plan for consistently adding money to this account. Each time you get paid from now on, pay yourself 10% of your income into this account. It's only 10%, but it will grow your savings and net worth more quickly than you might think.

You might doubt that you can pay all your bills if you are putting away 10%, but we have never seen anyone who couldn't make it happen. We have seen people cut their cable bill, reduce their soft drink purchases, and do a whole host of other things in order to grow their savings.

If you want your finances to change, you are going to need to change something about your finances. These two steps will make all the difference in your financial life and put you on the path to financial fitness.

Goal: I will start automatically paying myself 10% of my income into my YOU, Inc. Investment Hierarchy savings account by _____ .
                                                                              (date)
Completed: _____ .
                        (date)

Your Long-Term Vision

Now that you have a new savings account and a plan to increase it every time you get paid, how are you applying Principle 2? Specifically, what is your stewardship?

_____

_____

What is your mission in life?

_____

_____

What is your long-term vision and dream?

_____

_____

What do you want to do with your life stewardship?

_____

_____

And how much money will you need to effectively accomplish all of your dreams and plans?

$ _____

Take the time to answer these questions in writing. Unlike the fictional exercise earlier in this book about inheriting $10 million, this time your answers to the questions are real. This is your life. What do you want to do with it?

Take your stewardship seriously and fully write out your answers to the questions above. Write your long-term vision and dream. This matters. Knowing your stewardship, to your family and beyond, is an essential part of financial fitness. Knowing what you want to do with your life and what money you want and need in order to accomplish your goals is a vital part of getting in financial shape.

If you don't have a long-term vision, your money will naturally get frittered away. Successful people have a written financial plan. We want you to be financially successfully, so write out your vision.

What do you want to do, what do you want to spend your money on, and how much money do you want to spend on your stewardship? Give real effort and time to answering these questions in writing.

There are three things you can do with your money:
1. Acquire (things)
2. Accomplish (goals and dreams)
3. Contribute (to causes and people in need)

Continue this exercise of defining dreams and goals below. This is serious, but it can also be fun!

Things That You Would Like to Acquire:

If all cars cost only $1, what kinds would you buy? Be specific (model, color, year, etc.).

1. _____
2. _____
3. _____
4. _____
5. _____

If you could travel anywhere and stay as long as you wanted, where would you go?

1. _____
2. _____
3. _____
4. _____
5. _____

What are the attributes of your dream home (style, size, location, land, etc.)?

1. _____
2. _____
3. _____
4. _____
5. _____

What other "toys" (boats, vehicles, guns, gadgets, clothes, accessories, etc.) do you want?

1. _____
2. _____
3. _____
4. _____
5. _____

Goals and Dreams That You Would Like to Accomplish:

How much money do you want to have in your savings account?

$ _____

How old do you want to be when you are able to retire/be job optional?

_____

_____

How much debt do you want to have?

$ _____

What hobbies would you like to put more time and money into?

_____

_____

What kind of adventures would you like to go on? (Examples: race in the Baja 1,000, sail around the world, cage dive with great white sharks, get your pilot's license, take a motorcycle trip through 107 towns of Tuscany, etc.)

_____

_____

Who would you like to meet?

_____

_____

What things would you like to have more time to study and learn about?

_____

_____

Ways You Would Like to Contribute to Causes and People in Need:

To what charities would you like to contribute more time and money?

_____

_____

What activities would you like to have more time and money to spend doing with your family?

_____

_____

What causes would you like to see expanded with the help of your time and money?

_____

_____

Fill in these last lines with other dreams. Feel free to write more down on another piece of paper.

1. _____
2. _____
3. _____
4. _____
5. _____

* Activities:

Spend time "dream building" with friends and family. Go out and see, touch, smell, and experience all your different dreams. Test-drive the above cars. Tour through homes and properties like the ones written above. Look at brochures and online pictures of all your dreams. Create a dream/vision board. Get a large piece of poster board and place pictures of different dreams and goals that you would like to accomplish on it. The Internet and magazines are excellent resources for pictures. Place this board somewhere prominent in your home where you will see it frequently every day. If you are married and/or have children, make this into a family project. Create one board for each person and a shared one for the whole family.

Not only are these activities a lot of fun, but they will also help solidify your vision in your mind, serve as reminders of what you are running toward, and alert all of your senses and get your subconscious mind working full force toward success. Your hunger level for financial success will continue to rise.

CHAPTER FOUR

More on How to Begin Getting Financially Fit

PRINCIPLE 3: Live within your means. Always. No exceptions. Period. Follow a good budget. Give each spouse a small allowance so you have a little discretionary money each month and don't nitpick each other on the little things.

Take the time and go through all of the Financial Management Forms included with this book and create a plan for your finances.

Buy a box of legal-sized envelopes for the cash envelope system.

If you find yourself struggling to follow a budget, get a good financial advisor to help you and hold you accountable.

PRINCIPLE 4: Stop getting financial advice from broke people; get it only from those whose finances you want to emulate.

The List
Now, take a few minutes and make a list of people you have listened to on financial topics. Include family, friends, relatives, influential teachers, etc.

_____	_____
_____	_____
_____	_____
_____	_____
_____	_____
_____	_____

Once you have completed the list, use your pen or pencil to cross out every person whose finances you would not want to emulate. Circle those whose finances you would like to emulate.

From now on, weigh all financial advice using this same criterion. Keep this list and add to it over time as you hear counsel on finances from additional people.

Prepare Ahead

PRINCIPLE 5: Consistently budget and save for unexpected expenses.

Next, add an emergency fund to your budget. Your emergency fund is the second level of the YOU, Inc. Investment Hierarchy. Have the discipline to pay yourself first and fill in the hierarchy. As soon as possible, you need to get $1,000 into this account. This needs to be done *fast*—today! Sell your trading card collection, have a garage sale, skip meals, work extra hours, shovel a drive way, or mow a lawn. Do whatever it takes to get this done quickly! This will help you withstand some bumps in the road that may come along. Having the $1,000 will also naturally help you start thinking differently and seeing finances from a more secure perspective.

Murphy's Law predicts that unexpected expenses will come up. Even if you don't believe in this law, being prepared for the unexpected is wise counsel. The dog may get sick (probably from eating all that homework), the house may need sudden major repairs, a fender bender may send your car to the shop, or a car transmission might need to be replaced.

Budget for these expenses and others like them ahead of time. We suggest you open another (yes, another) savings account and put 10% of every income check or transfer you receive into this emergency savings fund. Then when the washer breaks, floods the entire basement, and ruins your luggage just before the big family trip, you will be ready to respond with minimal hardship.

Nobody really wants such unexpected expenses, but emergencies are inevitable. However, those with an emergency fund handle them with very little effort or concern. Being prepared provides great peace of mind in times of trouble. And having a special account specifically dedicated to your emergency fund will make you less likely to spend from it frivolously.

Goal: I will have at least $1,000 in my emergency fund by

_____.
              (date)

Completed: _____.
                        (date)

Just because incidents do not happen on a monthly basis, that does not mean they are emergencies. The emergency fund is for EMERGENCIES only. Determine if each item on the following list is a true emergency:

True Emergency	Not an Emergency	
☐	☐	Christmas gifts
☐	☐	Vacation
☐	☐	New tires and oil/lube for car
☐	☐	Back-to-school clothes
☐	☐	Checkups with the doctor/dentist
☐	☐	Firewood for fireplace
☐	☐	School supplies for yourself or child
☐	☐	New leather couch on sale
☐	☐	Uniform or gear for child who plays in a sport or participates in other extracurricular activities

Answers:

None of these are true emergencies. These should all be planned for as part of your budget. Things wear out. Christmas is the same time every year. If you fail to plan, you plan to fail.

Financial Management Forms

INTRODUCTION

Here is where we begin the wonderful world of cash flow management! We know, we know: you are so excited. Now if you are not a detailed personality, this may seem a bit intimidating at first, but do not worry. We will walk you through this, step by step.

By filling out just a few forms, your new financial plan will start to unfold right in front of you. You will also start to identify problem areas and learn how to plug up the holes of wasteful spending. You will have a new feeling of empowerment telling your money exactly where it needs to go!

The first time filling out these forms may take a little while. You may also have to face the brutal reality of the bad habits that have gotten you to this point. After this initial start-up, however, you will get better and better until cash flow management becomes second nature.

Complete the whole set of forms to get started. Then, you will only need to fill out the "Monthly Cash Flow Plan" (budget) once a month. This should only take about thirty minutes each month once you get in the habit. You will also want to update the whole set of forms every few months or whenever you experience a dramatic positive or negative financial event (like receiving an unexpected bonus or having to pay a large car repair bill).

The first form is a list of the major parts of a financial plan. This will help you set an action plan to get the ball rolling. This form is also a personal contract with yourself. This will help you get the mindset of a victor rather than a victim. Take full responsibility for your finances. Fill it out, and commit to your future. The forms after that will help you get a clear picture of where you are and also help prepare you for your Monthly Cash Flow Plan (budget).

Are you ready? Let's show those dollars who's the boss!

Financial Action Plan

	Action Needed	Goal Date	Date Accomplished
Written Cash Flow Plan	complete first budget	NOW	May 1
Debt Reduction Plan	begin debt roll-down	May 15	
Tax Reduction Plan	started business, meet CPA	June 1	
Emergency Savings Funding	open savings account	May 3	
Long-Term Savings Funding	open savings account	Aug 1	
Charitable Giving/Tithing	start tithing	May 15	
Dream/Vision Board	plan with family	May 10	
Personal Development	start a program	May 30	
Start My Business	done	NA	NA
Teach My Children	plan with wife	June 15	
Survival Preparation Planning	plan with wife	May 5	
Life Insurance	done	NA	NA
Health Insurance	done	NA	NA
Disability Insurance	NA	NA	NA
Auto Insurance	check current policy details	This week	
Homeowner's Insurance	check replacement cost	This week	
Will and/or Estate Planning	make appointment with lawyer	July 1	

I (We) _____ **Fred & Martha Snodgrass** _____, (a) responsible adult(s), do hereby promise to take full responsibility for my (our) financial future and to take the above declared actions by the stated dates to secure the well-being of my (our) family and myself (ourselves).

Signed: _____ *Fred Snodgrass* _____ Date: _____ May 1 _____

Signed: _____ *Martha Snodgrass* _____ Date: _____ May 1 _____

Financial Action Plan

	Action Needed	Goal Date	Date Accomplished
Written Cash Flow Plan	_____	_____	_____
Debt Reduction Plan	_____	_____	_____
Tax Reduction Plan	_____	_____	_____
Emergency Savings Funding	_____	_____	_____
Long-Term Savings Funding	_____	_____	_____
Charitable Giving/Tithing	_____	_____	_____
Dream/Vision Board	_____	_____	_____
Personal Development	_____	_____	_____
Start My Business	_____	_____	_____
Teach My Children	_____	_____	_____
Survival Preparation Planning	_____	_____	_____
Life Insurance	_____	_____	_____
Health Insurance	_____	_____	_____
Disability Insurance	_____	_____	_____
Auto Insurance	_____	_____	_____
Homeowner's Insurance	_____	_____	_____
Will and/or Estate Planning	_____	_____	_____

I (We) _____, (a) responsible adult(s), do hereby promise to take full responsibility for my (our) financial future and to take the above declared actions by the stated dates to secure the well-being of my (our) family and myself (ourselves).

Signed: _____ Date:_____

Signed: _____ Date:_____

Net Worth Statement

Item	Value	–	Debt	=	Equity
Real Estate _____	$150,000		$165,000		-$15,000
Real Estate _____					
Car _____ Mini Van _____	$15,000		$7,000		$5,000
Car _____ Truck _____	$7,000		$2,000		$5,000
Cash On Hand	$500				$500
Checking Account	$2,500				$2,500
Checking Account					
Savings Account	$1,700				$700
Money Market Account	$1,800				$1,800
Mutual Funds					
Retirement Plan	$3,200				$3,200
Gold/Silver	$2,100				$2,100
Insurance Cash Value					
Household Items	$7,500				$7,500
Jewelry					
Antiques					
Boat					
RV					
Credit Card Debt (negative)			$13,000		-$13,000
Unsecured Debt (negative)					
Other _ Sticky Wood Desk _	$100		$400		-$300
Other _____					
Other _____					
Other _____					
Total :	$191,400		$187,400		$4,000

Net Worth Statement

Item	Value	-	Debt	=	Equity
Real Estate_____	_____		_____		_____
Real Estate_____	_____		_____		_____
Car _____	_____		_____		_____
Car _____	_____		_____		_____
Cash On Hand	_____		_____		_____
Checking Account	_____		_____		_____
Checking Account	_____		_____		_____
Savings Account	_____		_____		_____
Money Market Account	_____		_____		_____
Mutual Funds	_____		_____		_____
Retirement Plan	_____		_____		_____
Gold/Silver	_____		_____		_____
Insurance Cash Value	_____		_____		_____
Household Items	_____		_____		_____
Jewelry	_____		_____		_____
Antiques	_____		_____		_____
Boat	_____		_____		_____
RV	_____		_____		_____
Credit Card Debt (negative)	_____		_____		_____
Unsecured Debt (negative)	_____		_____		_____
Other _____	_____		_____		_____
Other _____	_____		_____		_____
Other _____	_____		_____		_____
Other _____	_____		_____		_____
Total :	_____		_____		_____

Sources of Income

Source	Amount	When
Salary 1	$3,200	1st of the month
Salary 2	$900	1st & 15th - $450 each
Salary 3		
Bonus		
Business	$1,150	18th of the month
Pension		
Dividend Income		
Royalty Income		
Rents		
Side Jobs	$75	average per month
Alimony		
Child Support		
Unemployment		
Social Security		
Pension		
Annuity		
Disability Income		
Cash Gifts		
Trust Fund		
Other_____		
Other_____		
Other_____		
Total:	**$5,325**	

Sources of Income

Source	Amount	When
Salary 1	_____	_____
Salary 2	_____	_____
Salary 3	_____	_____
Bonus	_____	_____
Business	_____	_____
Pension	_____	_____
Dividend Income	_____	_____
Royalty Income	_____	_____
Rents	_____	_____
Side Jobs	_____	_____
Alimony	_____	_____
Child Support	_____	_____
Unemployment	_____	_____
Social Security	_____	_____
Pension	_____	_____
Annuity	_____	_____
Disability Income	_____	_____
Cash Gifts	_____	_____
Trust Fund	_____	_____
Other_____	_____	_____
Other_____	_____	_____
Other_____	_____	_____

Total: _____

Periodic Payment Planning

There are many kinds of common, recurring payments that do not come up every month. It is important to expect and plan for these and to not treat them as emergencies when they occur. Figure out the yearly amount of each item and divide it by twelve to determine how much should be set aside each month in your budget in order to cover these expenses.

Item	Annual Amount		Monthly Amount
Home Repairs/Maintenance	$1,500	/ 12 =	$125
Homeowner's Insurance		/ 12 =	
Property Taxes		/ 12 =	
Homeowners' Association Fees	$1,380	/ 12 =	$115
Replace Appliances		/ 12 =	
Replace Furniture		/ 12 =	
Medical Bills		/ 12 =	
Health Insurance		/ 12 =	
Life Insurance		/ 12 =	
Car Insurance		/ 12 =	
Car Repair/Registration	$3,000	/ 12 =	$250
Replace Car		/ 12 =	
Clothing	$400	/ 12 =	$34
School		/ 12 =	
Taxes (Self-Employed)		/ 12 =	
Vacation	$2,000	/ 12 =	$167
Gifts (birthdays, anniversary, etc.)		/ 12 =	
Christmas		/ 12 =	
Other_____		/ 12 =	
Other_____		/ 12 =	

Periodic Payment Planning

There are many kinds of common, recurring payments that do not come up every month. It is important to expect and plan for these and to not treat them as emergencies when they occur. Figure out the yearly amount of each item and divide it by twelve to determine how much should be set aside each month in your budget in order to cover these expenses.

Item	Annual Amount		Monthly Amount
Home Repairs/Maintenance	_____	/ 12 =	_____
Homeowner's Insurance	_____	/ 12 =	_____
Property Taxes	_____	/ 12 =	_____
Homeowners' Association Fees	_____	/ 12 =	_____
Replace Appliances	_____	/ 12 =	_____
Replace Furniture	_____	/ 12 =	_____
Medical Bills	_____	/ 12 =	_____
Health Insurance	_____	/ 12 =	_____
Life Insurance	_____	/ 12 =	_____
Car Insurance	_____	/ 12 =	_____
Car Repair/Registration	_____	/ 12 =	_____
Replace Car	_____	/ 12 =	_____
Clothing	_____	/ 12 =	_____
School	_____	/ 12 =	_____
Taxes (Self-Employed)	_____	/ 12 =	_____
Vacation	_____	/ 12 =	_____
Gifts (birthdays, anniversary, etc.)	_____	/ 12 =	_____
Christmas	_____	/ 12 =	_____
Other_____	_____	/ 12 =	_____
Other_____	_____	/ 12 =	_____

Monthly Cash Flow Plan/Budget Instructions

Every single dollar of your income should be allocated to some category on this form. When you are done, your total income minus expenses should equal zero. If it does not, then you need to adjust some categories (such as debt reduction, giving, or saving) so that it does equal zero. Use some common sense here, too. Do not leave things like clothes, car repairs, or home improvements off this list. If you do not plan for these things, then you are only setting yourself up for failure later.

Yes, we know this budget form is long. We tried to list practically every expense imaginable in order to prevent you from forgetting something. Do not expect to put something on every line item. Just use the ones that are relevant to your specific situation.

If there is a substantial difference between what you budgeted and what you spent, then you will need to readjust the budget to make up for the difference. If one category continually comes up over or short for two or three months, then you need to adjust the budgeted amount accordingly. Plan on remaking your budget each month since every month is different.

You will see three columns: Personal Expenses, Monthly Payment, and Balance. The Monthly Payment figure is your budgeted amount towards that item, even for the non-monthly expenses. The Balance column shows how much more you need to accumulate in order to be able to purchase the items that you are saving up for and how much you still owe on your debts. So some balances you want to grow, and others you want to shrink.

Also on the form is a place to track your emergency fund and long-term savings, as well as other savings plans you might already have, like a 401k.

Notes:
- An asterisk (*) beside an item indicates that it is an area for which it would be especially helpful to use the cash envelope system.
- Do not forget to include your annualized items from the "Periodic Payment Planning" sheet you filled out earlier, including your Christmas gift planning.
- Take the total income amount from the "Sources of Income" page and enter it in the Gross Monthly Income box. But also remember to write your take-home amount (after taxes) in the Net Monthly Income box. Don't fake yourself out. "Gross" is what you tell your friends. "Net" is what you tell your spouse.

Month: **September**

Monthly Cash Flow Plan

Personal Expenses	Monthly Payment	Balance
Tithing/Church/Charity	$900	
YOU, Inc. (at least 10% of income)	$900	
Personal Development Education	$210	
1st Mortgage Principal and Interest/Rent	$1,200	
2nd Mortgage or Credit Line		
Other Mortgage/Lien		
Property Tax (if not included)		
Hazard Insurance (if not included)		
Homeowners' Association Fees		
*Home Maintenance/Repairs	$50	$150
Electricity	$75	$150
Water (or Water/Sewer/Trash)	$62	
Sewer		
Trash		
Natural Gas	$32	
Telephone		
Cellular Phone	$120	
*Food/Groceries	$400	$400
Car Loan	$125	$4,200
Car Loan		
Other Vehicle Loan		
Gasoline	$210	
*Auto Maintenance/Repair	$200	$600
Car Insurance	$95	
*Auto Registration/License/Taxes	$21	$63
*Car Replacement		
*Medical Expenses	$25	$75
Medical Bills		
Health Insurance	$300	
Life Insurance	$63	
Alimony		
Child Support		
*Child Care		
*Baby Sitting		
*Baby Products		
*Clothing		
*Dry Cleaning/Laundry	$25	$35
Credit Card	$42	$3,500
Credit Card	$25	$1,800
Credit Card		
Credit Card		
Credit Card		
Student Loan		
Student Loan		
Other Loan		

Personal Expenses	Monthly Payment	Balance
*Christmas	$60	$180
*Gifts (birthdays, anniversary, etc.)	$10	$45
Organizational Dues		
Subscriptions		
*Toiletries	$40	$35
*Cosmetics	$30	$50
*Hair Care	$30	$50
*School Tuition		
*School Supplies		
*Pet Care		
*Lessons		
*Eating Out/Restaurants	$25	$30
*Replace Furniture	$20	$60
*Vacations	$60	$180
Internet	$25	
Cable/Satellite		
*Entertainment	$20	$20
*His Money to Blow	$40	
*Her Money to Blow	$60	
Other:_____		
Other:_____		
Other:_____		
Total Expenses:	**$5,500**	

Monthly Income

Gross Monthly Income	$9,000
Net Monthly Income (after taxes)	$5,500

Income Less Expenses	$0

(should be zero)

Savings	Amount	Value
Emergency Fund		$16,500
Long-Term Savings		$4,000
Gold (oz.)	3.25	$5,200
Silver (oz.)	204	$5,916
CD/Money Market		
401k/IRA/Retirement		
Stocks/Bonds		
Total:		**$31,616**

Month: _____

Monthly Cash Flow Plan

Personal Expenses	Monthly Payment	Balance	Personal Expenses	Monthly Payment	Balance
Tithing/Church/Charity			*Christmas		
YOU, Inc. (at least 10% of income)			*Gifts (birthdays, anniversary, etc.)		
Personal Development Education			Organizational Dues		
1st Mortgage Principal and Interest/Rent			Subscriptions		
2nd Mortgage or Credit Line			*Toiletries		
Other Mortgage/Lien			*Cosmetics		
Property Tax (if not included)			*Hair Care		
Hazard Insurance (if not included)			*School Tuition		
Homeowners' Association Fees			*School Supplies		
*Home Maintenance/Repairs			*Pet Care		
Electricity			*Lessons		
Water (or Water/Sewer/Trash)			*Eating Out/ Restaurants		
Sewer			*Replace Furniture		
Trash			*Vacations		
Natural Gas			Internet		
Telephone			Cable/Satellite		
Cellular Phone			*Entertainment		
*Food/Groceries			*His Money to Blow		
Car Loan			*Her Money to Blow		
Car Loan			Other:_____		
Other Vehicle Loan			Other:_____		
Gasoline			Other:_____		
*Auto Maintenance/Repair			**Total Expenses:**		
Car Insurance					
*Auto Registration/License/Taxes			**Monthly Income**		
*Car Replacement			Gross Monthly Income		
*Medical Expenses			Net Monthly Income (after taxes)		
Medical Bills					
Health Insurance			Income Less Expenses		
Life Insurance			(should be zero)		
Alimony					
Child Support					
*Child Care			**Savings**	**Amount**	**Value**
*Baby Sitting			Emergency Fund		
*Baby Products			Long-Term Savings		
*Clothing			Gold (oz.)		
*Dry Cleaning/Laundry			Silver (oz.)		
Credit Card			CD/Money Market		
Credit Card			401k/IRA/Retirement		
Credit Card			Stocks/Bonds		
Credit Card			**Total:**		
Credit Card					
Student Loan					
Student Loan					
Other Loan					

CHAPTER FIVE

How to Change Your Financial Habits

_____ is simple. Learn and follow the principles of financial fitness. The hardest part for most people is simply _____ _____.

There will always be another _____, but sticking to your _____ is the best deal of all.

_____ yourself and _____ your promises to yourself.

Techniques for Effective Change
1. The 24 Hour Rule: If you ever see a deal that is "too good to pass up," wait twenty-four hours before you buy.

2. Have an emergency fund. Note that your emergency fund is not for Christmas or good deals or other savings. It is for true emergencies. Don't touch it for any other purposes.

3. *Pay yourself first* and keep that money always. Get a separate savings account and pay 10% of everything you make to this account.

4. Make your payments to your savings and emergency fund automatic.

Techniques for Effective Financial Discipline
5. Cut up your credit cards, or freeze them in ice and leave them in the freezer so that even if you come to a moment of weakness, you will have to wait for them to thaw. (If you microwave them, they will be ruined.)

6. Set it up so that if you want to withdraw money from your bank, your financial mentor has to give approval and/or be present—especially for spontaneous purchases or uses of your emergency fund.

7. Keep close track of everything you spend.

8. If you are struggling with debt, communicate closely with your creditors. As long as you are paying them something, you are their asset. Communicate with those to whom you owe money and negotiate so they will keep working with you.

9. Renting a house can be a good idea for some people, especially when the economy is down because you won't have to ride a downward valuation slide. Also, this will save you the many costs of maintaining a home.

10. If needed, sell some of your stuff. This can feel hard at the time, but it helps get your mind in the right place when you sacrifice to achieve your new goals of financial fitness.

More Essential Techniques

11. Give yourself rewards for meeting your goals, such as going out to a movie if you stay within the budget all week. Use simple rewards and hold yourself to them.

Let's make some goals and rewards to work toward as you become more financially fit. Remember to make sure the rewards go with the goals and your current financial situation. Do not reward yourself with a trip to Hawaii just for starting your emergency fund. One type of a simple reward is what we call a "give up" reward. Pick something small that you really like, and are already doing, and decide to stop doing it until you reach your goal. For example, if you really like going out to the movies or eating a certain type of food, stop doing that until you reach your goal. Chris Brady once decided to stop drinking Diet Coke (which he really loved) until he hit a business goal. Make goals and rewards a habit.

Goal: Save $1,000 – Reward:_____

Goal: Start saving 10% – Reward:_____

Goal: Stick to budget for one month – Reward:_____

Goal: Stick to budget for three months – Reward:_____

Goal: Stick to budget for six months – Reward:_____

Goal: Have three months of expenses in savings – Reward:_____

Goal: Have six months of expenses in savings – Reward:_____

Goal: Have one year of expenses in savings – Reward:_____

Goal: Pay off a specific debt – Reward:_____

Goal: Be debt free (except for house) – Reward:_____

Business activity goal:_____ Reward:_____

Business results goal:_____ Reward:_____

12. Pay 10% of your income to tithing and give generously to charity and philanthropy. The spirit of giving is the spirit of abundance, and living in the attitude of abundance will bless you in many ways. That said, don't give to charity with the thought that by giving you will receive more. It can happen that way, but don't expect it. Give to help. Give even if you are really broke.

PRINCIPLE 6: Pay 10% of your income to tithing. Give even if you are really broke. Giving puts you in a mindset of abundance and puts any financial worries in their proper perspective, so it should not be limited to just tithing. The Bible categorizes giving as: 1. tithes and 2. offerings.

13. Know your purpose in life. Don't let money or the complications that come with it clutter your life. Focus on the goose that lays the golden eggs, meaning your work or business or other source of income, and not so much on what to do with the eggs.

14. Both spouses need to be on board. This is extremely important. In many relationships, one person is the natural spender, and the other is a natural saver. Do what it takes to work together to become financially fit.

Here are some tips for the Saver/Spender couple who are putting together a budget.

For Mr. or Mrs. Saver:

Write up the budget draft beforehand. Then, bring it to your spouse, have your say, and then shut up!

This should be a meeting, not a weekend seminar. The Spender's attention span only has about 15.5 minutes left.

You have to let the Spender mess with your budget! Oh no!

For Mr. or Mrs. Spender:

You must show up to the meeting!

You have to talk in the meeting. This means you must contribute mature input.

You need to change something on the Saver's budget draft.

You can never again say, "Whatever you want to do, honey."

CHAPTER SIX

Once You Have Started Doing the Basics, What's Next?

Many people don't have the _____ they could have because they are bogged down by their finances. Increased _____ allow you to more effectively pursue your life vision.

Take a moment and do the following exercise: List your top five problems. Write them down. Now look over the list and ask yourself how many of these problems could be solved if you had money in abundance. If having more money makes them go away, the problem itself isn't really the problem—*a lack of money* is.

PRINCIPLE 7: Using your time, money, and talents to genuinely help others naturally increases your happiness. Seeking money for money's sake may or may not influence your happiness, but seeking money in order to fulfill your stewardship and serve and bless others automatically increases it.

Take Action

Take a few moments right now to write out your plans to apply the principle covered in this chapter. List ways you might give more of your time, talents, and resources to help others and make a positive difference in your church, community, nation, and so on.

_____

_____

Summary of Part I—Basics

- Most people do not apply the principles of financial fitness and as a result, they constantly struggle with their finances. Our invitation to you is to be the exception, to join the few, the 5% who learn and apply the principles of financial success.
- Here are the basic, foundational principles of financial fitness covered in Part I:

  ▷ PRINCIPLE 1: It's not what you make but what you keep that determines financial success. Pay yourself first and save what you pay yourself.
  ▷ PRINCIPLE 2: Money is a gift. It has a specific use. This means that you have a stewardship. You are to use your money for something that matters, for your family and beyond.

▷ PRINCIPLE 3: Live within your means. Always. No exceptions. Period. Follow a good budget. Give each spouse a small allowance so you have a little discretionary money each month and don't nitpick each other on the little things.

▷ PRINCIPLE 4: Stop getting financial advice from broke people; get it only from those whose finances you want to emulate.

▷ PRINCIPLE 5: Consistently budget and save for unexpected expenses.

▷ PRINCIPLE 6: Pay 10% of your income to tithing. Give even if you are really broke. Giving puts you in a mindset of abundance and puts any financial worries in their proper perspective, so it should not be limited to just tithing. The Bible categorizes giving as: 1. tithes and 2. offerings.

▷ PRINCIPLE 7: Using your time, money, and talents to genuinely help others naturally increases your happiness. Seeking money for money's sake may or may not influence your happiness, but seeking money in order to fulfill your stewardship and serve and bless others automatically increases it.

• This book is designed not just for information but for *transformation*; each reader should outline in writing how he or she is going to implement these principles in everyday life.

• If you have skipped any of the assignments in this book or failed to write down your plan for each of the seven principles covered so far, stop right now and do these vitally important exercises. They will put you directly on the path of financial fitness.

• Once you are doing all seven of the basics, focus even more deeply and learn to master the basics. Make each of them a habit, an autopilot part of your life.

Fill in the blank key for Part I—Basics:

KNOWING, ACTION, MONEY, FINANCIAL, FITNESS, MONEY, PRIORITIES, BASICS, CHANGE, WORLD, INFORMATIONAL, TRANSFORMATIONAL, IMPLEMENT, SUCCESS, GETTING, STARTED, DEAL, BUDGET, INSPIRE, HONOR, INFLUENCE, RESOURCES

PART II

OFFENSE

"MOVE THE CHAINS!"

CHAPTER SEVEN

Moneyviews

An attitude of _____ is central to financial fitness.

Money is a _____ of your life purpose.

Money becomes a dangerous or productive _____ depending on the heart that wields it.

Choose Your Moneyview
1. Money as a Mystery
2. Money as a Master
3. Money as a Monster
4. Money as a Major
5. Money as a Motivator
6. Money as a Manipulator
7. Money as a Minimizer
8. Money as a Maximizer
9. Money as a Monument
10. Money as a Menace

Part of becoming financially fit consists of wisely choosing the right moneyview. Successful people adopt the Money as a Maximizer view, even if they were raised with other perspectives. As you consider this list of popular moneyviews, it may be helpful to ask yourself the following questions:

Which moneyview best represents where you are *right now?*

_____

_____

Which of these moneyviews have you encountered in the lives of other people in your life?

_____

_____

Which have you followed for a period of time in your life?

_____

_____

Notice that several of these views are quite negative. What are you doing to make sure you have a positive and productive moneyview?

_____

_____

PRINCIPLE 8: People with the right moneyview discipline themselves to live the principles of financial fitness, make financial decisions based on a long-term vision, adopt the habit of delayed gratification, and use the compounding nature of money to constructively achieve their dreams.

Etch It in Stone!

Think deeply about the moneyview or moneyviews you had as you began reading this book. Write it or them down. Now, write down the view or views you would like to attain. What are you committed to doing in order to make this change? Record this and prepare to make it real.

CHAPTER EIGHT

Invest in Yourself

Investing in _____ is the best investment you will ever make.

A first step in the attitude of _____ is to always remember that your most important investment is an investment in _____.

Whatever you do, don't cut back on _____ investment.

PRINCIPLE 9: Financially fit people are avid readers and consistently invest in themselves by increasing their financial and leadership education, skills, experience, knowledge, and ability.

In addition to studying and applying the material in this book, list ways you can invest in yourself and create a significantly improved you. How can you invest in your leadership education and experience? In your financial wisdom? In your skills, knowledge, and abilities? How can you become an even more avid reader?

What mentors do you need? What advice from current mentors do you need to follow more closely?

_____

_____

Are you currently on a self-directed educational path of reading, listening, and associating? Yes / No

If so, list out the types of personal and leadership development education that you are pursuing. If not, then write down some areas in which you would like to improve.

_____

_____

Why is reading important to growing your leadership influence and increasing your financial fitness?

_____

_____

Fill in the blanks below to create a plan of self-improvement:

I will read _____ books this year.
             (number)

Possible titles:_____

_____

_____

I will read _____ books this month.
             (number)

I will read (or am reading) the following books:

_____

_____

Why are attending seminars/conferences and listening to audio/watching video recordings important to growing your leadership influence and increasing your financial fitness?

_____

_____

I will listen to/watch _____ recordings this year, which can be broken down as:
                        (number)

_____ per month,

_____ per week, and

_____ per day.

I will listen to the following recordings:

_____

_____

I will attend _____ seminars/conferences this year.
              (number)

I will attend _____ seminars/conferences per month.
              (number)

The next seminar/conference I will attend is:

_____
                    (name, date, and location)

Do you already have access to an ongoing, credible educational program that provides leadership and personal development materials? If not, or you would like to learn about different options, the authors have provided recommendations at the back of this workbook.

PRINCIPLE 10: Financially fit people excel at the work and projects they are doing now, and at the same time, they invest in themselves in order to achieve their long-term vision.

What can you do to apply this principle? How can you truly excel—at a whole new level—in your current responsibilities?

_____

_____

CHAPTER NINE

Make Money Your Servant, Not Your Master

Your prosperity, wealth, and privileges are not ultimately for your _____ but for your _____.

_____ is not reality. Reality is reality.

Success is not as easy as _____ make it look, but it is also not as hard as _____ make it seem.

PRINCIPLE 11: Never sacrifice principles for money or possessions. Be honest. Keep your integrity. Keep your priorities in the right order.

In the past, have you sacrificed your principles for money or possessions? Starting now, what are some key principles that you vow to never sacrifice?

_____

_____

PRINCIPLE 12: Do the work to gain mastery in what you do (usually about 10,000 hours).

What is your current focus of mastery?

_____

_____

If you put in the 10,000 hours to master what you are currently doing, will you be able to accomplish your long-term vision and dreams? Yes/No Where can you focus to get even better?

_____

_____

If not, write down some ideas of things that can lead you to your long-term vision and dreams.

_____

_____

CHAPTER TEN

The Power of Multipliers

Albert Einstein said that _____ interest is the eighth wonder of the world.

Do you have _____ working for you or against you?

"If we're not sure, the answer is '_____.' If we're sure, let's _____ and see." —Orrin Woodward

There's waste in _____.

_____ the habits that don't serve you well, and _____ habits that are in keeping with your life purpose and bring you what you really want.

PRINCIPLE 13: Financially fit people don't ask "Can we afford it?" as much as they ask: "Do we *really* want this? Will it help our purpose and dream? *How* will it help our purpose and dream? In what ways might it be a distraction? Will it cost more money to take care of it or keep it (through things like insurance or annual fees)? Would saving or investing the same amount be a bigger help to our purpose and vision? Is now the best time for this purchase, or would it be less expensive or just better for our family or business at a later date?" They cultivate a habit of saying "No" to purchases even when they can easily afford them and of putting much of their money into savings or investments instead.

PRINCIPLE 14: Financially fit people analyze their habits—in life as well as finances—and work to break bad habits and cultivate good ones. They think about and choose the habits they want and need to achieve their life dreams.

CHAPTER ELEVEN

Two Great Financial Keys: Spending Habits and Passive Income

The number one influence on whether or not a couple becomes millionaires is the spending habits of the _____.

PRINCIPLE 15: Own a business, even if you start out working on it part-time. You can apply all the other principles in this book and obtain wealth over time, but those who apply them in their own businesses can become wealthy much more quickly.

*Action Step:

Consult with a tax professional to learn about the different ways you can benefit from the business owner tax code.

PRINCIPLE 16: Increase your passive income to the point that 1. most of your income is passive and 2. you can live off your passive income.

PRINCIPLE 17: Retirement should not be an issue of age but rather a function of having enough passive income to live on for life. Retirement means retiring from things that are not part of your purpose so you can focus your productive work on your life mission.

In your own words, what is the difference between active and passive income?

_____

_____

List all of your sources of income and classify each as active or passive.

_____

_____

Do you need to find a passive income to pursue, grow your current one, or both?

_____

_____

CHAPTER TWELVE

Stop Chasing Money and Chase Your Purpose

"What would you do if you weren't _____?" —Shannon Alder

The first key to _____ is in making everything work for your life purpose.

It's okay to feel _____ at times. It's just not okay to stay that way.

Even the most brilliant of us are often _____ when we leave our area of expertise, and we would nearly always be better off financially if we remained within our area of expertise and used everything we had to increase our mastery and feed the _____ _____!

How many days could you live your current lifestyle if you stopped working? Take a few minutes, look over your spending records, and figure this out.

_____

_____

Three Keys to Wealth

Robert Kiyosaki says there are three keys to wealth: 1. long-term vision, 2. delayed gratification, and 3. the power of compounding.

If your long-term vision isn't clear and you get a financial windfall of some kind, say $5,000, it will be gone very quickly and you will have little to show for it—because you will be tempted to follow the Spending Multiplier rather than the Investment Multiplier. A fool and his money are soon parted, as Benjamin Franklin predicted. In truth, 93% of people who win the lottery lose it all very quickly.

On the other hand, if you have a clear life vision and financial plan, you will think about the best ways to build your pipeline and move toward your dream, and the $5,000 will enable you to take a significant leap forward.

If you came into an extra $5,000, what would your plan for this money be? Could it help the investment in yourself? Could you fill up your emergency fund sooner than planned? Develop a plan now for what to do if some extra cash comes into your life.

_____

_____

Building Momentum

How much money do you need to be free (meaning that your passive income is enough to live on and you can work full-time building your business and living your purpose)? You need to know this number.

$ _____

PRINCIPLE 18: To really attain financial success, focus on these things: 1. Truly excel in your current job and projects and simultaneously start a business; 2. Put in the 10,000 or so hours needed to gain mastery over your business while still excelling at your current job; 3. Make a plan to become financially free by reaching a point where the passive income from your business more than covers your family's needs; 4. Once you are financially free, put your full-time focus on building your business to the point that it funds your life purpose. Each of these requires deep focus, one at a time. Once you have accomplished one of them, go to the next and give it the same level of focus.

Identify which of these four is your current needed focus and develop a strategy to make it happen. Add it (in writing) to your previous plans and update them so you have a detailed outline of what to concentrate on as you accomplish the next item on the list. Put your plan into action.

CHAPTER THIRTEEN

Choosing Your Business

What are your _____, and how can you build your business around them?

PRINCIPLE 19: Get good mentors and really listen to them.

Write Down the Pros and Cons

If you are already a successful business system owner, ask yourself:

> Do you want to start another business system, or grow the one you already own?

> Do you want to build a new business system from scratch?

> Or do you want to buy into a business system opportunity that is already established—so you can focus on growth?

Have you gained mastery in your current business field?

Do you want to buy a business system outside your area of mastery and take the time to gain a new mastery?

Or do you want to buy another business system within your field of mastery?

Is it time to grow your business system while you continue focusing on your dream?

Or is it time to sell your business system, or perhaps hire a CEO to run it, and focus more on your dream?

How can you connect your business system to your passions?

If you are not already a successful business system owner, consider the following:

You probably don't want to buy an existing business system, unless you have a lot of experience in the field, such as from working in a family business. Do you have mastery in this business field?

Do you have access to the funding to buy the existing company?

Are you interested in a franchise?

Do you have access to the resources needed to purchase a franchise?

Have you looked into networking companies and found one that resonates with your passions and interests?

Do you want to build a business system from scratch?

Can you excel more in your current job, so you can bring in increased resources to build your business system?

What are your passions and how can you build your business system around them?

Do you have passion for a business system idea but need leadership experience and resources in order to do something about it? If so, do you need a first-tier business system that gives you experience and money for a few years?

In what areas do you want to gain mastery, and are you willing to put in the necessary time in order to do so? And what business system opportunities are available in these arenas?

Who will mentor you?

CHAPTER FOURTEEN

Feed the Golden Goose!

Does the _____ result in a return, or is it gone forever?

It seems few people have ever been taught that _____ has a purpose beyond its use toward their immediate comfort and _____.

It is the _____ to use money _____ that separates the wealthy from the rest.

_____ are rarely the solution. Extremes rarely work.

The way to dig yourself out of an economic _____ is to figure out what your _____ is (or find one) and feed that goose.

If you have to _____ your _____, it isn't time to play.

You are your best _____. Invest in _____, and invest effectively and wisely in building your business.

PRINCIPLE 20: Use your money productively—by putting it where it will bring you back more than you put in—rather than nonproductively. The best investment is in yourself and your own business. Wisely and appropriately use some of your savings to increase your business assets and returns.

Update your financial plan to include putting more of your money to productive use, and consider when to use some of your bank account savings in more productive business uses that increase your rate of return.

Warning: Do not take this step until you have built up adequate savings and your business is ready to significantly benefit from the additional assets. Only use this money to fund assets that will bring bigger returns than you put in. Do not use savings to speculate. Only invest this way in your own business, something under your control. Consult your mentor as you make these decisions.

CHAPTER FIFTEEN

The Investment Hierarchy

Investing in you is the _____ focus of good investment.

Saving for a worst case includes the opposite of _____ money, which we will call "_____."

7. SPECULATIVE VENTURES, START-UPS, INVENTIONS

6. STOCK MARKET, REAL ESTATE

5. CDS, MONEY MARKET ACCOUNTS, MUNICIPAL BONDS

4. SAVINGS (BOTH LONG-TERM AND TARGETED)

3. SURVIVAL PREPARATION

2. EMERGENCY FUND (3-6 MONTHS OF EXPENSES)

1. YOURSELF

What have you done to invest into Level One (Yourself)?

_____

_____

How much money do you have in Level Two (Emergency Fund)?

$ _____

Do you at least have a $1,000 beginning emergency fund? Yes/No

PRINCIPLE 21: Put some money into preparing for a worst-case scenario. Don't be fanatical about this, but don't ignore it either.

What money and other items do you already have set aside for worst-case scenarios?

_____

_____

Make a list of things that should eventually be added to this level of the YOU, Inc. Investment Hierarchy (certain amount of cash, food storage, water, batteries, lights, 72-hour kits, silver coins, guns, ammo, etc.):

_____

_____

PRINCIPLE 22: Build up a regular targeted savings fund for things you want to buy later. Consistently fund this account and buy consumer items with cash (not financing).

Are you already saving for something specific? If so, what? How much money have you saved toward this purchase?

_____

_____

PRINCIPLE 23: Only invest money you can afford to lose entirely in speculations outside your area(s) of mastery. Only invest a little, if any, in such ventures.

PRINCIPLE 24: Do not ever use your savings to speculate.

Make a plan and a commitment now of what to do when an "investment opportunity" comes your way.

_____

Summary of Part II—Offense

- Financial offense means taking action to increase your income. This is the first focus of financial fitness beyond the basics because it emphasizes the attitudes of abundance, leadership, innovation, and entrepreneurialism.
- The principles of financial offense covered in Part II are:

▷ PRINCIPLE 8: People with the right moneyview discipline themselves to live the principles of financial fitness, make financial decisions based on a long-term vision, adopt the habit of delayed gratification, and use the compounding nature of money to constructively achieve their dreams.

▷ PRINCIPLE 9: Financially fit people are avid readers and consistently invest in themselves by increasing their financial and leadership education, skills, experience, knowledge, and ability.

▷ PRINCIPLE 10: Financially fit people excel at the work and projects they are doing now, and at the same time, they invest in themselves in order to achieve their long-term vision.

▷ PRINCIPLE 11: Never sacrifice principles for money or possessions. Be honest. Keep your integrity. Keep your priorities in the right order.

▷ PRINCIPLE 12: Do the work to gain mastery in what you do (usually about 10,000 hours).

▷ PRINCIPLE 13: Financially fit people don't ask "Can we afford it?" as much as they ask: "Do we *really* want this? Will it help our purpose and dream? *How* will it help our purpose and dream? In what ways might it be a distraction? Will it cost more money to take care of it or keep it (through things like insurance or annual fees)? Would saving or investing the same amount be a bigger help to our purpose and vision? Is *now* the best time for this purchase, or would it be less expensive or just better for our family or business at a later date?" They cultivate a habit of saying "No" to purchases even when they can easily afford them and of putting much of their money into savings or investments instead.

▷ PRINCIPLE 14: Financially fit people analyze their habits—in life as well as finances—and work to break bad habits and cultivate good ones. They think about and choose the habits they want and need to achieve their life dreams.

▷ PRINCIPLE 15: Own a business, even if you start out working on it part-time. You can apply all the other principles in this book and obtain wealth over time, but those who apply them in their own businesses can become wealthy much more quickly.

▷ PRINCIPLE 16: Increase your passive income to the point that 1. most of your income is passive and 2. you can live off your passive income.

▷ PRINCIPLE 17: Retirement should not be an issue of age but rather a function of having enough passive income to live on for life. Retirement means retiring from things that are not part of your purpose so you can focus your productive work on your life mission.

▷ PRINCIPLE 18: To really attain financial success, focus on these things: 1. Truly excel in your current job and projects and simultaneously start a business; 2. Put in the 10,000 or so hours needed to gain mastery over your business while still excelling at your current job; 3. Make a plan to become financially free by reaching a point where the passive income from your business more than covers your family's needs; and 4. Once you are financially free, put your full-time focus on building your business to the point that it funds your life purpose. Each of these requires deep focus, one at a time. Once you have accomplished one of them, go to the next and give it the same level of focus.

▷ PRINCIPLE 19: Get good mentors and really listen to them.

▷ PRINCIPLE 20: Use your money productively—by putting it where it will bring you back more than you put in—rather than nonproductively. The best investment is in yourself and your own business. Wisely and appropriately use some of your savings to increase your business assets and returns.

▷ PRINCIPLE 21: Put some money into preparing for a worst-case scenario. Don't be fanatical about this, but don't ignore it either.

▷ PRINCIPLE 22: Build up a targeted savings fund for things you want to buy later. Consistently fund this account and buy consumer items with cash (not financing).

▷ PRINCIPLE 23: Only invest money you can afford to lose entirely in speculations outside your area(s) of mastery. Only invest a little, if any, in such ventures.

▷ PRINCIPLE 24: Do not ever use your savings to speculate.

• Be sure to stop and consider how to use all of these principles in your life, and add them to your written financial plan.

Fill in the blank key for Part II—Offense:

ABUNDANCE, MAXIMIZER, TOOL, YOU, ABUNDANCE, YOURSELF, BRAIN, PLEASURE, PURPOSE, PERCEPTION, WINNERS, LOSERS, COMPOUND, INTEREST, NO, WAIT, HASTE, REJECT, CULTIVATE, WIFE, AFRAID, WEALTH, DEFEATED, IDIOTS, GOLDEN, GOOSE, PASSIONS, EXPENSE, MONEY, GRATIFICATION, DISCIPLINE, PRODUCTIVLEY, EXTREMES, PROBLEM, GOOSE, FINANCE, RECREATION, ASSET, YOU, FIRST, COMPOUNDING, IMPOUNDING

PART III

DEFENSE

"GET THE QUARTER BACK!"

CHAPTER SIXTEEN

Myths about Debt

The key is to _____ for things right now. Pay as you go.

PRINCIPLE 25: Get rid of debt.

PRINCIPLE 26: If you aren't financially sound, don't get caught in the trap of using "business debt."

PRINCIPLE 27: Do not use credit cards to build your credit because this almost always leads people to more debt.

PRINCIPLE 28: Never use title pawning, "ninety-days-same-as-cash" loans, payday loans, rent-to-own plans, layaway debt, or similar schemes.

PRINCIPLE 29: See your car(s) as transportation, not status symbols. Save up and always pay cash for them.

1. The average millionaire purchases a _____ car.
   a) three-year-old   c) two-year-old
   b) new   d) one-year-old

2. The average millionaire has a _____ monthly car payment.
   a) $300   c) $450
   b) $650   d) $0

Answers
   1. c) The average millionaire purchases a <u>two-year-old</u> car.
   2. d) The average millionaire has a <u>$0</u> monthly car payment.

PRINCIPLE 30: Debit cards are better than credit cards for many people, and cash is even better.

PRINCIPLE 31: Teach your children and youth the principles of financial fitness. Set the example for them. Mentoring them will help you as well as them.

PRINCIPLE 32: If you are not wealthy, do not get sucked in to using second mortgages.

CHAPTER SEVENTEEN

Getting Out of Debt

"A budget is not a line drawn in the sand. It is a _____ _____."
—Kristine Militello

"More money doesn't fix the problem until you really _____ your finances and take charge of them." —Marc Militello

PRINCIPLE 33: Use the roll-down method to pay off all credit card debts and then apply it to all other debts.

You may not need to sell anything to get your debt roll-down program going, but think about what you could sell to get a little extra money in a short time period. List ten things you could sell fairly quickly through a garage sale or online advertising. Think of items you are not using or no longer see a need to keep.

1. _____
2. _____
3. _____
4. _____
5. _____
6. _____
7. _____
8. _____
9. _____
10. _____

Debt Roll-Down Instructions

Let's get ready to eradicate this cancer called debt! The idea of the debt roll-down method is simple: Because of the high interest, start with your consumer debt, especially credit cards. List them in order from the smallest balance to the largest. If there is a choice between two low-balance cards, pay the one with the highest interest off first. The goal is to get rid of the clutter of all the smallest payments and kill off the easiest debts first. Decide on a fixed percentage or amount of money that you are able to add every month to your minimum debt payments and make this as automatic as possible.

If you receive any windfalls of cash or unexpected income, add it to the lowest balance card. Sell things from your garage or storage, or other things you do not need. The goal is to knock out the balance on the card as quickly as possible.

Once you have paid off the first card, keep the same amount going toward the card with the next lowest balance. Give this a similar focus and pay off this card as soon as possible. To be clear, every time you pay a card off, you add what you were paying on that card to the next card payment. So, as you pay off a debt and roll down the payment to the next one, you pick up momentum. Continue to do the same with each card until all of your credit card debt is gone. At that point, apply this same roll-down method to your other debts, starting with those that have the highest interest rates.

The sample form shows a list of debts in order from the smallest to the largest balance. The total amount of minimum payments equals $440. Once the first card has been paid off, the $20 that was being paid to that debt gets added to the second debt payment. The new payment (which is always the total of the previous debts' payments plus the current debt's payment) for the second debt is now $60, and $440 is still paid toward the total debt. The sample below shows what your form will look like as debts are paid off.

Without the debt roll-down method, it would take you thirteen years to pay off these debts, and you would pay $7,139 in interest. Using the debt roll-down method, it would take you only *two years and nine months* to pay them off, and you would *save $3,890 in interest*!

This example shows only the minimum payments. Imagine how much faster this roll-down method could go if a set amount of money was added every month. If an extra $50 a month was added to this example, it would be paid off in two years and six months and would save you $4,275 in interest. With an extra $100 every month, it would be paid off in two years and three months and would save you $4,578 in interest. And adding an extra $200 every month would enable you to pay it off in one year and ten months while saving almost $5,000 in interest.

Every time you pay off a debt, scratch it out. Keep this paper so you can see your victories and how close you are to getting rid of this cancer!

Debt Roll-Down

Item	Total Payoff	Minimum Payment	Interest Rate	New Payment
Department Store	$500	$20	18%	$20
Furniture Store	$1,000	$40	22%	$60
MasterCard	$2,000	$80	19%	$140
American Express	$3,000	$120	19%	$260
Visa	$4,500	$180	20%	

Debt Roll-Down

Item	Total Payoff	Minimum Payment	Interest Rate	New Payment
_____	_____	_____	_____	_____
_____	_____	_____	_____	_____
_____	_____	_____	_____	_____
_____	_____	_____	_____	_____
_____	_____	_____	_____	_____
_____	_____	_____	_____	_____
_____	_____	_____	_____	_____
_____	_____	_____	_____	_____
_____	_____	_____	_____	_____
_____	_____	_____	_____	_____
_____	_____	_____	_____	_____
_____	_____	_____	_____	_____
_____	_____	_____	_____	_____
_____	_____	_____	_____	_____
_____	_____	_____	_____	_____
_____	_____	_____	_____	_____

CHAPTER EIGHTEEN

Don't Be Normal

Normal people are _____. Don't be normal where finances are concerned.

Reduce your _____ to make life less complicated.

Accumulate wisdom faster than _____.

If you're right with _____, who else do you really need to impress?

PRINCIPLE 34: Learn to be skeptical of advertising, media, and marketing.

PRINCIPLE 35: Accumulate slowly; build your inventory of resources and wisdom, not stuff.

*Action Step:

Take a walk through your garage/storage area and see what "stuff" you can get rid of to reduce clutter and maybe get some extra money.

PRINCIPLE 36: Get right with God, apply true principles in all areas of life including finances, pursue your stewardship, serve others—and leave impressing others in God's hands.

PRINCIPLE 37: Do not use consumer debt. Wise financing for business investment may be okay at times, but consumer debt is like a cancer. Cut it out!

If you have consumer debt, how is your debt roll-down plan going? How much consumer debt do you now have?

_____

_____

PRINCIPLE 38: Make memories part of your lifestyle, budget, and life plan. Start simple and add big memories, too.

Name two of your top memories with your family and/or friends. What made them special?

_____

_____

Plan on doing something within the next twenty-four hours that significantly adds to your memories.

_____

_____

Write down at least two big memory-building activities you are planning to do within the next twelve months.

_____

_____

CHAPTER NINETEEN

Ten Financial Danger Zones

PRINCIPLE 39: Be very, very careful as you make decisions about the danger zones: taxes, home ownership, divorce, credit cards, lawsuits, insurance, seeking status, college, addictions, and investments. Get good advice from your financial mentors, and study things in detail before taking action.

Have you been "burned" with one or more of these danger zones? If so, which ones?

_____

_____

Are you currently approaching or involved in one or more of these areas? Which one(s)? Tread lightly!

_____

_____

CHAPTER TWENTY

What It Means to Deserve

Never finance anything that _____ (aside from your home).

PRINCIPLE 40: If you buy a home, follow the 2X Rule. For example, if your income is $50,000 per year, do not buy a home that costs more than $100,000. If you want a bigger home, earn more money.

How much is your annual income?
$ _____

According to the 2X Rule, what's the maximum amount your home should cost? $
$ _____

If you own a home, how much is your current home mortgage?
$ _____

If you are renting your home, your monthly rental costs should be no more than 25-35% of your net, take-home income. What is your monthly take-home pay?
$ _____

How much is your monthly rent?
$ _____

What percentage of your take-home pay is your rent?_____%

PRINCIPLE 41: If you are not financially fit and you have a bunch of "toys," it means that you do not really deserve them and you are using your savings or debt on the wrong things. If your debts are all paid off, you are following the savings guidelines listed in earlier principles, and you have the cash, you can buy a few "toys" and still be financially fit.

Summary of Part III—Defense
- The principles of financial defense include:

  ▷ PRINCIPLE 25: Get rid of debt.
  ▷ PRINCIPLE 26: If you aren't financially sound, don't get caught in the trap of using "business debt."

▷ PRINCIPLE 27: Do not use credit cards to build your credit because this almost always leads people to more debt.

▷ PRINCIPLE 28: Never use title pawning, "ninety-days-same-as-cash" loans, payday loans, rent-to-own plans, layaway debt, or similar schemes.

▷ PRINCIPLE 29: See your car(s) as transportation, not status symbols. Save up and always pay cash for them.

▷ PRINCIPLE 30: Debit cards are better than credit cards for many people, and cash is even better.

▷ PRINCIPLE 31: Teach your children and youth the principles of financial fitness. Set the example for them. Mentoring them will help you as well as them.

▷ PRINCIPLE 32: If you are not wealthy, do not get sucked in to using second mortgages.

▷ PRINCIPLE 33: Use the roll-down method to pay off all credit card debts and then apply it to all other debts.

▷ PRINCIPLE 34: Learn to be skeptical of advertising, media, and marketing.

▷ PRINCIPLE 35: Accumulate slowly; build your inventory of resources and wisdom, not stuff.

▷ PRINCIPLE 36: Get right with God, apply true principles in all areas of life including finances, pursue your stewardship, serve others—and leave impressing others in God's hands.

▷ PRINCIPLE 37: Do not use consumer debt. Wise financing for business investment may be okay at times, but consumer debt is like a cancer. Cut it out!

▷ PRINCIPLE 38: Make memories part of your lifestyle, budget, and life plan. Start simple and add big memories, too.

▷ PRINCIPLE 39: Be very, very careful as you make decisions about the danger zones: taxes, home ownership, divorce, credit cards, lawsuits, insurance, seeking status, college, addictions, and investments. Get good advice from your financial mentors, and study things in detail before taking action.

▷ PRINCIPLE 40: If you buy a home, follow the 2X Rule. For example, if your income is $50,000 per year, do not buy a home that costs more than $100,000. If you want a bigger home, earn more money.

▷ PRINCIPLE 41: If you are not financially fit and you have a bunch of "toys," it means that you do not really deserve them and you are using your savings or debt on the wrong things. If your debts are all paid off, you are following the savings guidelines listed in earlier principles, and you have the cash, you can buy a few "toys" and still be financially fit.

Fill in the blank key for Part III—Defense:

PAY, STONE, WALL, UNDERSTAND, BROKE, STUFF, WIDGETS, GOD, DEPRECIATES

PART IV

PLAYING FIELD

"NOT IN OUR HOUSE!"

CHAPTER TWENTY-ONE

The First Three Great Economic Questions

People living in free-enterprise economies experience higher levels of _____ and _____.

This is one of the repeating patterns of history: Every government eventually seeks to _____ its _____.

Constitutions are superior to _____, and all laws in truly free nations must adhere to the _____.

When free enterprise _____, the obstacles to financial fitness always _____.

PRINCIPLE 42: Studying and understanding free enterprise is an essential part of financial fitness.

What is your plan to study freedom and free enterprise?

_____

_____

PRINCIPLE 43: Financially fit people who want to maintain an environment that encourages opportunity and prosperity pay attention to the principles of freedom and the ongoing actions of government.

Have you noticed your local and national governments creeping toward a command economy? If so, in what ways?

_____

_____

CHAPTER TWENTY-TWO

The Fourth Great Economic Question: Is the Economy as Good as Gold?

_____ is the only currency that has proven able to accomplish all of the important traits of good money.

PRINCIPLE 44: In addition to cash savings, save some of your money in something other than fiat currency.

How much gold or silver do you have?

_____

_____

What is your plan to acquire some?

_____

_____

CHAPTER TWENTY-THREE

A Brief History of Gold

Investing in metals is analogous to _____ _____.

PRINCIPLE 45: Study up on investments in metal, and any other investment, before you buy. Do your homework. Take your time.

Do you already have a knowledge of gold and other precious metals? If so, teach others. If not, what is your plan to learn more about this?

_____

_____

CHAPTER TWENTY-FOUR

The Fifth Great Economic Question: What Is Your Enterprise?

The collective, individually chosen _____ of a nation of free people is one of the most powerful forces in all _____ history.

PRINCIPLE 46: Invest even more in yourself by learning to be the kind of person who consistently engages in an enterprising, creative, enthusiastic type of life. Fill your days with enterprise, action, and doing things that matter. And teach your children and the people you work with to do the same. Become the kind of person and leader who consistently works on your current enterprise.

CHAPTER TWENTY-FIVE

The Camel in the Tent

If _____ are given the _____ to act, they will bring more affluence to the nations where they work.

Do you know the history of your nation's monetary system? How far is the camel inside the tent?

_____

_____

What is your plan to help get the stinky animal outside?

_____

_____

What is your financial plan if he gets all the way in (or even if he is already all the way in)?

_____

_____

CHAPTER TWENTY-SIX

Prepare for the Future

The core principles of _____ _____ are directly applicable to big institutions and _____ as well.

Most successful _____—and _____—follow a similar pattern.

Financial fitness means living the kind of life that brings _____ success; it is not a "get-rich-quick" scheme, but a _____ focus on effective financial principles.

PRINCIPLE 47: Study the strengths and/or weaknesses of your nation and economy (and others where you do business) and wisely consider and prepare for potential economic downturns.

How is your YOU, Inc. Investment Hierarchy coming along? How have you been investing in yourself?

_____

_____

Have you started a business yet? Yes/No If not, what are your plans to start one?

_____

_____

How much do you have in your emergency fund?

$ _____

How is your survival savings and preparation coming along?

_____

_____

Aside from a home mortgage, how much debt do you have left?

$ _____

Do you have any money in your long-term savings yet? Yes/No If so, how much?

$ _____

What local meeting(s) will you attend this month to get to know your community and build relationships? (Examples: political district meeting, home owners association meeting for your neighborhood, "meet up" groups, open business workshop, church social event, etc.)

_____

_____

_____

_____

_____

Summary of Part IV—Playing Field

- The principles covered in this section include:

  ▷ PRINCIPLE 42: Studying and understanding free enterprise is an essential part of financial fitness.
  ▷ PRINCIPLE 43: Financially fit people who want to maintain an environment that encourages opportunity and prosperity pay attention to the principles of freedom and the ongoing actions of government.
  ▷ PRINCIPLE 44: In addition to cash savings, save some of your money in something other than fiat currency.
  ▷ PRINCIPLE 45: Study up on investments in metal, and any other investment, before you buy. Do your homework. Take your time.
  ▷ PRINCIPLE 46: Invest even more in yourself by learning to be the kind of person who consistently engages in an enterprising, creative, enthusiastic type of life. Fill your days with enterprise, action, and doing things that matter. And teach your children and the people you work with to do the same. Become the kind of person and leader who consistently works on your current enterprise.
  ▷ PRINCIPLE 47: Study the strengths and/or weaknesses of your nation and economy (and others where you do business) and wisely consider and prepare for potential economic downturns.

- Get serious about studying finances, freedom, and economics.

Fill in the blank key for Part IV—Playing Field:

FREEDOM, PROSPERITY, INCREASE, POWER, LAWS, CONSTITUTION, DECLINES, INCREASE, GOLD, FREEZING, FRUIT, ENTERPRISE, HUMAN, ENTREPRENEURS, FREEDOM, PERSONAL, FINANCE, GOVERNMENTS, PEOPLE, NATIONS, ECONOMIC, LONG-TERM

CONCLUSION

If you do this, you are going to look back on this day as a _____
_____ in your life.

It is amazing how simple it really is to get _____ _____,
and yet so many people do not bother to do it. Be different!

Are you one of the _____, entrepreneurs, and dreamers who will step
up to the plate and swing for the fences? The _____ needs you to be
financially fit. It's time to take a stand!

Name five people with whom you will share these principles and this program
in order to help their personal financial fitness and to help you strengthen your
community with this knowledge.
1.
2.
3.
4.
5.

Fill in the blank key for Conclusion:
TURNING, POINT, FINACIALLY, FIT, LEADERS, WORLD

Financial Management Forms

INTRODUCTION

Here is where we begin the wonderful world of cash flow management! We know, we know: you are so excited. Now if you are not a detailed personality, this may seem a bit intimidating at first, but do not worry. We will walk you through this, step by step.

By filling out just a few forms, your new financial plan will start to unfold right in front of you. You will also start to identify problem areas and learn how to plug up the holes of wasteful spending. You will have a new feeling of empowerment telling your money exactly where it needs to go!

The first time filling out these forms may take a little while. You may also have to face the brutal reality of the bad habits that have gotten you to this point. After this initial start-up, however, you will get better and better until cash flow management becomes second nature.

Complete the whole set of forms to get started. Then, you will only need to fill out the "Monthly Cash Flow Plan" (budget) once a month. This should only take about thirty minutes each month once you get in the habit. You will also want to update the whole set of forms every few months or whenever you experience a dramatic positive or negative financial event (like receiving an unexpected bonus or having to pay a large car repair bill).

The first form is a list of the major parts of a financial plan. This will help you set an action plan to get the ball rolling. This form is also a personal contract with yourself. This will help you get the mindset of a victor rather than a victim. Take full responsibility for your finances. Fill it out, and commit to your future. The forms after that will help you get a clear picture of where you are and also help prepare you for your Monthly Cash Flow Plan (budget).

Are you ready? Let's show those dollars who's the boss!

Financial Action Plan

	Action Needed	Goal Date	Date Accomplished
Written Cash Flow Plan	complete first budget	NOW	May 1
Debt Reduction Plan	begin debt roll-down	May 15	
Tax Reduction Plan	started business, meet CPA	June 1	
Emergency Savings Funding	open savings account	May 3	
Long-Term Savings Funding	open savings account	Aug 1	
Charitable Giving/Tithing	start tithing	May 15	
Dream/Vision Board	plan with family	May 10	
Personal Development	start a program	May 30	
Start My Business	done	NA	NA
Teach My Children	plan with wife	June 15	
Survival Preparation Planning	plan with wife	May 5	
Life Insurance	done	NA	NA
Health Insurance	done	NA	NA
Disability Insurance	NA	NA	NA
Auto Insurance	check current policy details	This week	
Homeowner's Insurance	check replacement cost	This week	
Will and/or Estate Planning	make appointment with lawyer	July 1	

I (We) _____ **Fred & Martha Snodgrass** _____, (a) responsible adult(s), do hereby promise to take full responsibility for my (our) financial future and to take the above declared actions by the stated dates to secure the well-being of my (our) family and myself (ourselves).

Signed: _____ *Fred Snodgrass* _____   Date: _____ May 1 _____

Signed: _____ *Martha Snodgrass* _____   Date: _____ May 1 _____

Financial Action Plan

	Action Needed	Goal Date	Date Accomplished
Written Cash Flow Plan	_____	_____	_____
Debt Reduction Plan	_____	_____	_____
Tax Reduction Plan	_____	_____	_____
Emergency Savings Funding	_____	_____	_____
Long-Term Savings Funding	_____	_____	_____
Charitable Giving/Tithing	_____	_____	_____
Dream/Vision Board	_____	_____	_____
Personal Development	_____	_____	_____
Start My Business	_____	_____	_____
Teach My Children	_____	_____	_____
Survival Preparation Planning	_____	_____	_____
Life Insurance	_____	_____	_____
Health Insurance	_____	_____	_____
Disability Insurance	_____	_____	_____
Auto Insurance	_____	_____	_____
Homeowner's Insurance	_____	_____	_____
Will and/or Estate Planning	_____	_____	_____

I (We) _____, (a) responsible adult(s), do hereby promise to take full responsibility for my (our) financial future and to take the above declared actions by the stated dates to secure the well-being of my (our) family and myself (ourselves).

Signed: _____ Date:_____

Signed: _____ Date:_____

Net Worth Statement

Item	Value	-	Debt	=	Equity
Real Estate_____	$150,000		$165,000		-$15,000
Real Estate_____					
Car _____Mini Van_____	$15,000		$7,000		$5,000
Car _____Truck_____	$7,000		$2,000		$5,000
Cash On Hand	$500				$500
Checking Account	$2,500				$2,500
Checking Account					
Savings Account	$1,700				$700
Money Market Account	$1,800				$1,800
Mutual Funds					
Retirement Plan	$3,200				$3,200
Gold/Silver	$2,100				$2,100
Insurance Cash Value					
Household Items	$7,500				$7,500
Jewelry					
Antiques					
Boat					
RV					
Credit Card Debt (negative)			$13,000		-$13,000
Unsecured Debt (negative)					
Other Sticky Wood Desk	$100		$400		-$300
Other_____					
Other_____					
Other_____					
Total :	$191,400		$187,400		$4,000

Net Worth Statement

Item	Value	-	Debt	=	Equity
Real Estate_____	_____		_____		_____
Real Estate_____	_____		_____		_____
Car _____	_____		_____		_____
Car _____	_____		_____		_____
Cash On Hand	_____		_____		_____
Checking Account	_____		_____		_____
Checking Account	_____		_____		_____
Savings Account	_____		_____		_____
Money Market Account	_____		_____		_____
Mutual Funds	_____		_____		_____
Retirement Plan	_____		_____		_____
Gold/Silver	_____		_____		_____
Insurance Cash Value	_____		_____		_____
Household Items	_____		_____		_____
Jewelry	_____		_____		_____
Antiques	_____		_____		_____
Boat	_____		_____		_____
RV	_____		_____		_____
Credit Card Debt (negative)	_____		_____		_____
Unsecured Debt (negative)	_____		_____		_____
Other _____	_____		_____		_____
Other _____	_____		_____		_____
Other _____	_____		_____		_____
Other _____	_____		_____		_____
Total :	_____		_____		_____

Sources of Income

Source	Amount	When
Salary 1	$3,200	1st of the month
Salary 2	$900	1st & 15th - $450 each
Salary 3		
Bonus		
Business	$1,150	18th of the month
Pension		
Dividend Income		
Royalty Income		
Rents		
Side Jobs	$75	average per month
Alimony		
Child Support		
Unemployment		
Social Security		
Pension		
Annuity		
Disability Income		
Cash Gifts		
Trust Fund		
Other_____		
Other_____		
Other_____		
Total:	$5,325	

Sources of Income

Source	Amount	When
Salary 1	_____	_____
Salary 2	_____	_____
Salary 3	_____	_____
Bonus	_____	_____
Business	_____	_____
Pension	_____	_____
Dividend Income	_____	_____
Royalty Income	_____	_____
Rents	_____	_____
Side Jobs	_____	_____
Alimony	_____	_____
Child Support	_____	_____
Unemployment	_____	_____
Social Security	_____	_____
Pension	_____	_____
Annuity	_____	_____
Disability Income	_____	_____
Cash Gifts	_____	_____
Trust Fund	_____	_____
Other_____	_____	_____
Other_____	_____	_____
Other_____	_____	_____
Total:	_____	

Periodic Payment Planning

There are many kinds of common, recurring payments that do not come up every month. It is important to expect and plan for these and to not treat them as emergencies when they occur. Figure out the yearly amount of each item and divide it by twelve to determine how much should be set aside each month in your budget in order to cover these expenses.

Item	Annual Amount		Monthly Amount
Home Repairs/Maintenance	$1,500	/ 12 =	$125
Homeowner's Insurance		/ 12 =	
Property Taxes		/ 12 =	
Homeowners' Association Fees	$1,380	/ 12 =	$115
Replace Appliances		/ 12 =	
Replace Furniture		/ 12 =	
Medical Bills		/ 12 =	
Health Insurance		/ 12 =	
Life Insurance		/ 12 =	
Car Insurance		/ 12 =	
Car Repair/Registration	$3,000	/ 12 =	$250
Replace Car		/ 12 =	
Clothing	$400	/ 12 =	$34
School		/ 12 =	
Taxes (Self-Employed)		/ 12 =	
Vacation	$2,000	/ 12 =	$167
Gifts (birthdays, anniversary, etc.)		/ 12 =	
Christmas		/ 12 =	
Other_____		/ 12 =	
Other_____		/ 12 =	

Periodic Payment Planning

There are many kinds of common, recurring payments that do not come up every month. It is important to expect and plan for these and to not treat them as emergencies when they occur. Figure out the yearly amount of each item and divide it by twelve to determine how much should be set aside each month in your budget in order to cover these expenses.

Item	Annual Amount		Monthly Amount
Home Repairs/Maintenance	_____	/ 12 =	_____
Homeowner's Insurance	_____	/ 12 =	_____
Property Taxes	_____	/ 12 =	_____
Homeowners' Association Fees	_____	/ 12 =	_____
Replace Appliances	_____	/ 12 =	_____
Replace Furniture	_____	/ 12 =	_____
Medical Bills	_____	/ 12 =	_____
Health Insurance	_____	/ 12 =	_____
Life Insurance	_____	/ 12 =	_____
Car Insurance	_____	/ 12 =	_____
Car Repair/Registration	_____	/ 12 =	_____
Replace Car	_____	/ 12 =	_____
Clothing	_____	/ 12 =	_____
School	_____	/ 12 =	_____
Taxes (Self-Employed)	_____	/ 12 =	_____
Vacation	_____	/ 12 =	_____
Gifts (birthdays, anniversary, etc.)	_____	/ 12 =	_____
Christmas	_____	/ 12 =	_____
Other_____	_____	/ 12 =	_____
Other_____	_____	/ 12 =	_____

Monthly Cash Flow Plan/Budget Instructions

Every single dollar of your income should be allocated to some category on this form. When you are done, your total income minus expenses should equal zero. If it does not, then you need to adjust some categories (such as debt reduction, giving, or saving) so that it does equal zero. Use some common sense here, too. Do not leave things like clothes, car repairs, or home improvements off this list. If you do not plan for these things, then you are only setting yourself up for failure later.

Yes, we know this budget form is long. We tried to list practically every expense imaginable in order to prevent you from forgetting something. Do not expect to put something on every line item. Just use the ones that are relevant to your specific situation.

If there is a substantial difference between what you budgeted and what you spent, then you will need to readjust the budget to make up for the difference. If one category continually comes up over or short for two or three months, then you need to adjust the budgeted amount accordingly. Plan on remaking your budget each month since every month is different.

You will see three columns: Personal Expenses, Monthly Payment, and Balance. The Monthly Payment figure is your budgeted amount towards that item, even for the non-monthly expenses. The Balance column shows how much more you need to accumulate in order to be able to purchase the items that you are saving up for and how much you still owe on your debts. So some balances you want to grow, and others you want to shrink.

Also on the form is a place to track your emergency fund and long-term savings, as well as other savings plans you might already have, like a 401k.

Notes:
- An asterisk (*) beside an item indicates that it is an area for which it would be especially helpful to use the cash envelope system.
- Do not forget to include your annualized items from the "Periodic Payment Planning" sheet you filled out earlier, including your Christmas gift planning.
- Take the total income amount from the "Sources of Income" page and enter it in the Gross Monthly Income box. But also remember to write your take-home amount (after taxes) in the Net Monthly Income box. Don't fake yourself out. "Gross" is what you tell your friends. "Net" is what you tell your spouse.

Month: September

Monthly Cash Flow Plan

Personal Expenses	Monthly Payment	Balance	Personal Expenses	Monthly Payment	Balance
Tithing/Church/Charity	$900		*Christmas	$60	$180
YOU, Inc. (at least 10% of income)	$900		*Gifts (birthdays, anniversary, etc.)	$10	$45
Personal Development Education	$210		Organizational Dues		
1st Mortgage Principal and Interest/Rent	$1,200		Subscriptions		
2nd Mortgage or Credit Line			*Toiletries	$40	$35
Other Mortgage/Lien			*Cosmetics	$30	$50
Property Tax (if not included)			*Hair Care	$30	$50
Hazard Insurance (if not included)			*School Tuition		
Homeowners' Association Fees			*School Supplies		
*Home Maintenance/Repairs	$50	$150	*Pet Care		
Electricity	$75	$150	*Lessons		
Water (or Water/Sewer/Trash)	$62		*Eating Out/Restaurants	$25	$30
Sewer			*Replace Furniture	$20	$60
Trash			*Vacations	$60	$180
Natural Gas	$32		Internet	$25	
Telephone			Cable/Satellite		
Cellular Phone	$120		*Entertainment	$20	$20
*Food/Groceries	$400	$400	*His Money to Blow	$40	
Car Loan	$125	$4,200	*Her Money to Blow	$60	
Car Loan			Other: _____		
Other Vehicle Loan			Other: _____		
Gasoline	$210		Other: _____		
*Auto Maintenance/Repair	$200	$600	**Total Expenses:**	$5,500	
Car Insurance	$95				
*Auto Registration/License/Taxes	$21	$63	**Monthly Income**		
*Car Replacement			Gross Monthly Income		$9,000
*Medical Expenses	$25	$75	Net Monthly Income (after taxes)		$5,500
Medical Bills					
Health Insurance	$300		Income Less Expenses		$0
Life Insurance	$63				(should be zero)
Alimony					
Child Support					
*Child Care			**Savings**	**Amount**	**Value**
*Baby Sitting			Emergency Fund		$16,500
*Baby Products			Long-Term Savings		$4,000
*Clothing			Gold (oz.)	3.25	$5,200
*Dry Cleaning/Laundry	$25	$35	Silver (oz.)	204	$5,916
Credit Card	$42	$3,500	CD/Money Market		
Credit Card	$25	$1,800	401k/IRA/Retirement		
Credit Card			Stocks/Bonds		
Credit Card				**Total:**	$31,616
Credit Card					
Student Loan					
Student Loan					
Other Loan					

Month: _____

Monthly Cash Flow Plan

Personal Expenses	Monthly Payment	Balance	Personal Expenses	Monthly Payment	Balance
Tithing/Church/Charity			*Christmas		
YOU, Inc. (at least 10% of income)			*Gifts (birthdays, anniversary, etc.)		
Personal Development Education			Organizational Dues		
1st Mortgage Principal and Interest/Rent			Subscriptions		
2nd Mortgage or Credit Line			*Toiletries		
Other Mortgage/Lien			*Cosmetics		
Property Tax (if not included)			*Hair Care		
Hazard Insurance (if not included)			*School Tuition		
Homeowners' Association Fees			*School Supplies		
*Home Maintenance/Repairs			*Pet Care		
Electricity			*Lessons		
Water (or Water/Sewer/Trash)			*Eating Out/ Restaurants		
Sewer			*Replace Furniture		
Trash			*Vacations		
Natural Gas			Internet		
Telephone			Cable/Satellite		
Cellular Phone			*Entertainment		
*Food/Groceries			*His Money to Blow		
Car Loan			*Her Money to Blow		
Car Loan			Other:_____		
Other Vehicle Loan			Other:_____		
Gasoline			Other:_____		
*Auto Maintenance/Repair			**Total Expenses:**		
Car Insurance					
*Auto Registration/License/Taxes			**Monthly Income**		
*Car Replacement			Gross Monthly Income		
*Medical Expenses			Net Monthly Income (after taxes)		
Medical Bills					
Health Insurance			Income Less Expenses		
Life Insurance			(should be zero)		
Alimony					
Child Support					
*Child Care			**Savings**	**Amount**	**Value**
*Baby Sitting			Emergency Fund		
*Baby Products			Long-Term Savings		
*Clothing			Gold (oz.)		
*Dry Cleaning/Laundry			Silver (oz.)		
Credit Card			CD/Money Market		
Credit Card			401k/IRA/Retirement		
Credit Card			Stocks/Bonds		
Credit Card			Total:		
Credit Card					
Student Loan					
Student Loan					
Other Loan					

Debt Roll-Down Instructions

Let's get ready to eradicate this cancer called debt! The idea of the debt roll-down method is simple: Because of the high interest, start with your consumer debt, especially credit cards. List them in order from the smallest balance to the largest. If there is a choice between two low-balance cards, pay the one with the highest interest off first. The goal is to get rid of the clutter of all the smallest payments and kill off the easiest debts first. Decide on a fixed percentage or amount of money that you are able to add every month to your minimum debt payments and make this as automatic as possible.

If you receive any windfalls of cash or unexpected income, add it to the lowest balance card. Sell things from your garage or storage, or other things you do not need. The goal is to knock out the balance on the card as quickly as possible.

Once you have paid off the first card, keep the same amount going toward the card with the next lowest balance. Give this a similar focus and pay off this card as soon as possible. To be clear, every time you pay a card off, you add what you were paying on that card to the next card payment. So, as you pay off a debt and roll down the payment to the next one, you pick up momentum. Continue to do the same with each card until all of your credit card debt is gone. At that point, apply this same roll-down method to your other debts, starting with those that have the highest interest rates.

The sample form shows a list of debts in order from the smallest to the largest balance. The total amount of minimum payments equals $440. Once the first card has been paid off, the $20 that was being paid to that debt gets added to the second debt payment. The new payment (which is always the total of the previous debts' payments plus the current debt's payment) for the second debt is now $60, and $440 is still paid toward the total debt. The sample below shows what your form will look like as debts are paid off.

Without the debt roll-down method, it would take you thirteen years to pay off these debts, and you would pay $7,139 in interest. Using the debt roll-down method, it would take you only *two years and nine months* to pay them off, and you would *save $3,890 in interest*!

This example shows only the minimum payments. Imagine how much faster this roll-down method could go if a set amount of money was added every month. If an extra $50 a month was added to this example, it would be paid off in two years and six months and would save you $4,275 in interest. With an extra $100 every month, it would be paid off in two years and three months and would save you $4,578 in interest. And adding an extra $200 every month would enable you to pay it off in one year and ten months while saving almost $5,000 in interest.

Every time you pay off a debt, scratch it out. Keep this paper so you can see your victories and how close you are to getting rid of this cancer!

Debt Roll-Down

Item	Total Payoff	Minimum Payment	Interest Rate	New Payment
Department Store	$500	$20	18%	$20
Furniture Store	$1,000	$40	22%	$60
MasterCard	$2,000	$80	19%	$140
American Express	$3,000	$120	19%	$260
Visa	$4,500	$180	20%	

Debt Roll-Down

Item	Total Payoff	Minimum Payment	Interest Rate	New Payment

LIFE SERIES

Our lives are lived out in the eight categories of Faith, Family, Finances, Fitness, Following, Freedom, Friends, and Fun. The monthly LIFE Series of 4 audios and 1 book is specifically designed to bring you life-transforming information in each of these areas. Whether you are interested in one or two of these, or all eight, you will be delighted with timeless truths and effective strategies for living a life of excellence, brought to you in an entertaining, intelligent, well-informed, and insightful manner. It has been said that it may be your life, but it's not yours to waste. Subscribe to the LIFE Series today and learn how to make yours count!

The LIFE Series – dedicated to helping people grow in each of the 8 F categories: Faith, Family, Finances, Fitness, Following, Freedom, Friends, and Fun.
4 audios and 1 book are shipped each month.
$50.00 plus S&H
Pricing is valid for both USD and CAD.

LLR SERIES

Everyone will be called upon to lead at some point in life—and often at many points. The question is whether people will be ready when they are called. The LLR Series is based on the *New York Times* bestseller *Launching a Leadership Revolution*, in which authors Chris Brady and Orrin Woodward teach about leadership in a way that applies to everyone. Whether you are seeking corporate or business advancement, community influence, church impact, or better stewardship and effectiveness in your home, the principles and specifics taught in the LLR Series will equip you with what you need.

Subscribers receive 4 audios and 1 leadership book each month. Topics covered include finances, leadership, public speaking, attitude, goal setting, mentoring, game planning, accountability and progress tracking, levels of motivation, levels of influence, and leaving a personal legacy.

Subscribe to the LLR Series and begin applying these life-transforming truths today!

The LLR (Launching a Leadership Revolution) Series – dedicated to helping people grow in their leadership ability.
4 audios and 1 book are shipped each month.
$50.00 plus S&H
Pricing is valid for both USD and CAD.

AGO SERIES

Whether you have walked with Christ your entire life or have just begun the journey, we welcome you to experience the love, joy, understanding, and purpose that only Christ can offer. This series is designed to touch and nourish the hearts of all faith levels. Gain valuable support and guidance from our top speakers and special guests that will help you enhance your understanding of God's plan for your life, marriage, children, and character. Nurture your soul, strengthen your faith, and find answers on the go or quietly at home with the AGO Series.

The AGO (All Grace Outreach) Series – dedicated to helping people grow spiritually.
1 audio and 1 book are shipped each month.
$25.00 plus S&H
Pricing is valid for both USD and CAD.

EDGE SERIES

Designed especially for those on the younger side of life, this is a hard-core, no-frills approach to learning the things that make for a successful life.

Eliminate the noise around you about who you are and who you should become. Instead, figure it out for yourself in a mighty way with life-changing information from people who would do just about anything to have learned these truths much, much sooner in life. Get access on a monthly basis to wisdom and knowledge that it took them a lifetime to discover!

Edge Series – dedicated to helping young people grow in their leadership ability.
1 audio is shipped each month.
$10.00 plus S&H
Pricing is valid for both USD and CAD.

FREEDOM SERIES

Attention all freedom lovers: Gain an even greater understanding of the significance and power of freedom, stay informed about the issues that affect your own freedom, and find out what you can do to reverse any decline and lead the world toward greater liberty with the LIFE Freedom Series!

Freedom Series – dedicated to helping people understand the meaning and value of freedom.
1 audio is shipped each month.
$10.00 plus S&H
Pricing is valid for both USD and CAD.

LIFE LIBRARY

The LIFE Library is your round-the-clock resource for LIFE's latest and greatest leadership content in either video or audio format. And you never have to be quiet in this library!

WATCH, LISTEN, LEARN, AND GROW!

- Audio and video content covering LIFE's 8 Fs (Faith, Family, Finances, Fitness, Following, Freedom, Friends, and Fun)

- New exclusive content added every month

- Material from industry leaders, including bestselling authors Orrin Woodward and Chris Brady and LIFE Coaches Tim Marks and Claude Hamilton

- Option to read reviews and share your own insights

- Ability to create a list of favorites for quick and easy retrieval

- A feature that allows you to search by format, speaker, and/or subject

$40.00 per month
Pricing is valid for both USD and CAD.

RASCAL RADIO

Listen up! You asked for it, and we heard you loud and clear. Now hear this: Rascal Radio is a one-of-a-kind, personal-development Internet radio hot spot. Switch on and tune in to an incredible selection of preset stations for each of LIFE's 8 Fs that you can customize by choosing a combination of speaker or subject matter. The life-changing possibilities are endless as you browse through the hundreds of audio recordings available. Select and purchase your favorite talks to gift to family and friends. Listen, learn, and grow through the ease of Rascal Radio.

Subscription includes a 7-Day FREE Trial.
$49.95 per month

Now Available:
FREE Rascal Radio Smartphone App!

LIFE LIVE

The dynamic, world-class LIFE Live educational events are designed to inform, equip, and train you for success in a powerful way.

Ranging in size from a couple hundred to thousands of participants all across North America, these fun, energy-packed events deliver life-changing information from LIFE's 8 F categories (Faith, Family, Finances, Fitness, Following, Freedom, Friends, and Fun).

$40.00 per month
Pricing is valid for both USD and CAD.

ALL GRACE
OUTREACH

All Grace Outreach originally began in 1993 in Maine as Christian Mission Services. In March of 2007, the organization was transferred to Michigan, and the name was changed to All Grace Outreach. All Grace Outreach is a 501(c)(3) charitable organization (which means all contributions are tax deductible) and is committed to providing assistance to those in need. Our main focus is spreading the gospel of Jesus Christ throughout the world and helping abused, abandoned, and distressed children and widows.

Mission and Vision: To impact and improve the lives of children both locally and globally and to fund Christian outreach efforts throughout the world.

Here is a partial list of the organizations your donation supports:

Founders Ministries
A New Beginning Pregnancy Center
PLNTD
GAP Ministries
Wisdom for the Heart
Samaritan's Purse
Milwaukee Rescue Mission
Ligonier Ministries
Shepherds Theological Seminary
Zoie Sky Foundation
Catholic Christian Outreach
Italy for Christ

allgraceoutreach.com

NOTES

Notes

NOTES

NOTES